THE RAILWAYS OF DERBYSHIRE

PATRICK BENNETT

AMBERLEY

First published 2022

Amberley Publishing
The Hill, Stroud
Gloucestershire, GL5 4EP

www.amberley-books.com

Copyright © Patrick Bennett, 2022

The right of Patrick Bennett to be identified as
the Author of this work has been asserted in
accordance with the Copyrights, Designs and
Patents Act 1988.

ISBN 978 1 3981 1009 0 (print)
ISBN 978 1 3981 1010 6 (ebook)

British Library Cataloguing in Publication Data.
A catalogue record for this book is available from
the British Library.

Typesetting by SJmagic DESIGN SERVICES, India.
Printed in the UK.

Introduction

Derbyshire is a county of contrasts, in its geology as much as in its economy and industry, and indeed these three aspects are closely linked. From the heart of the county at Derby sprang out the lines of the three founder companies of the Midland Railway, east to Nottingham, west to Birmingham, north to Leeds and south towards London. In the east of the county were the coalfields, a battleground fought over by four different railway companies: the Midland, the Great Northern, the Great Central, and the Lancashire Derbyshire and East Coast Railway. This intense rivalry led to a complex mesh of lines with, in places, small villages having railway stations provided by three different railway companies.

The limestone geology at the centre of the county proved a challenge for the Midland's drive to complete its line to Manchester. It also gave rise to the London and North Western's Cromford & High Peak Railway, a line built primarily for the extraction of limestone. Further north the Midland forced a route through both limestone and millstone grit to connect Sheffield and Manchester via the Hope Valley Line. Further north still, and much earlier, the Great Central had built its line through the Longdendale Valley and Woodhead Tunnel to join Manchester and Sheffield; a modernised, electrified line that was closed far too early.

In the south of the county the Great Northern, with running powers over its ally the North Staffordshire, manged to complete a route from Nottingham to Stafford. At the heart of the county is Derby, the headquarters of the Midland, and a great engineering centre, as indeed it remains today. It is a city of considerable historical interest.

The author and publisher would like to thank the following people/organisations for permission to use copyright material in this book: The Science Museum, The Railway Correspondence and Travel Society, J.W. Sutherland, Eastbank Model Railway Club. The photographs by Phil Sangwell, Ben Brooksbank, Dave Bevis, The Jeyes, Geoffrey Skelsey, Martin Addison, and Walter Dendy are reproduced under the Creative Commons Attribution Share-alike license 2.0. Every attempt has been made to seek permission for copyright material used in this book. However, if we have inadvertently used copyright material without permission/acknowledgement, we apologise and will make the necessary correction at the first opportunity.

The Midland Railway

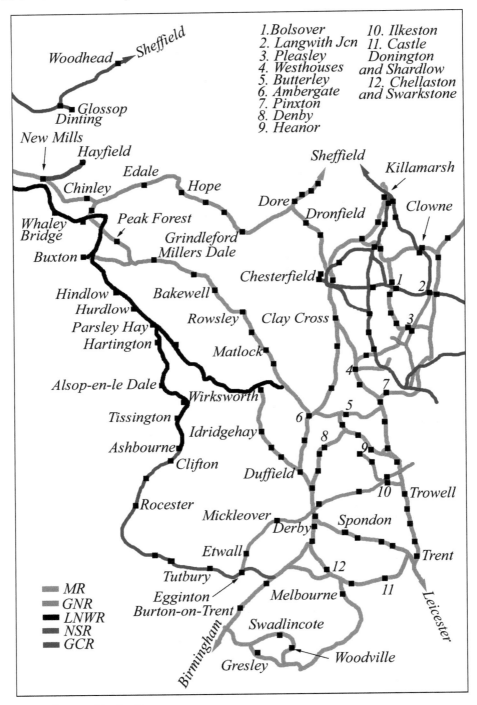

The railways of Derbyshire.

The North Midland Railway

An Act of 4 July 1836 authorised the North Midland Railway to build a line from Leeds to Derby. The engineer for the line was George Stephenson, who, because of his aversion to steep gradients, decided that the line would run via Rotherham, thus bypassing the important town of Sheffield, which would be served by a branch from Masborough. The major engineering work on the line was the construction of the 1-mile-long Clay Cross tunnel. The line opened on 1 July 1840. An East Midlands Trains Class 222 'Meridian' unit emerges from the northern portal of the tunnel on 21 May 2010. (Phil Sangwell)

The first station north from Derby was Derby Nottingham Road, opened on 1 September 1856. One of its main purposes was the transport of personnel and horses for the nearby Derby Racecourse. This is a view looking south, with a freight train passing on the Down Goods. The station closed in 1967.

Seen from a road bridge just to the north of Duffield station is a Hughes-Fowler 2-6-0 'Crab' with a Class D freight on the Up Fast. In the background a Down freight is entering the 855-yard Milford tunnel. The photograph was taken on 15 June 1957 by Ben Brooksbank.

Ambergate station has had a complicated history. The first station opened with the railway in 1840. The opening of the southern spur of the Miller's Dale line led to the station being moved south. The Ambergate to Pye Bridge line opened in 1875 and in the following year a loop to the west of the main line completed a triangular layout at the station. Subsequent developments led to the closure of this station and the building of a single platform station on the line to Matlock. This is the original station building, designed by Francis Thompson. To the right is Toadmoor Tunnel.

Right: The quadrupling of the tracks south of Ambergate in 1931 led to the opening out of Longlands Tunnel, the work in progress seen here. (Science Museum)

Below: Wingfield is the only surviving station of the twenty-four designed by Francis Thompson for the North Midland Railway. For this reason and for its architectural merit it is listed Grade ll*. The station closed in 1967 and for some years has been in poor condition. It has recently been purchased by Amber Valley Borough Council and work is now under way to restore it to its original condition.

At Clay Cross North Junction the Erewash Valley line is joined. On 7 April 1988 Class 20s Nos 20196 and 20182 are seen hauling failed Class 47 No. 47448 with the 07.20 Harwich Parkeston Quay to Manchester Piccadilly 'Boat Train'. At this point the train was running one hour forty-eight minutes late.

A nice shot of Chesterfield station in 1956, small boys no doubt waiting for their next 'cop'. On the right a Class 4F 0-6-0 is lurking on the goods lines. (Phil Sangwell)

On 18 September 1981 Class 45 'Peak' No. 45056 pulls away from Chesterfield with the 07.00 Bristol to Leeds. Between 1962 and 1983, when they were replaced by HSTs, these Class 45s hauled almost all expresses on the Midland main line.

Just north of Chesterfield station is a footbridge, a favourite haunt of railway photographers. On 27 September 1963 4F 0-6-0 No. 44586 is seen on the Up Fast with a Class H goods train. (Ben Brooksbank)

Travelling in the opposite direction on 18 September 1981, Class 40 No. 40082 with a train of HTV hopper wagons switches from Down Fast to Down Slow in order to take the Barrow Hill line at Tapton Junction.

Whittington station was opened in 1861. It was replaced by a new station further north in 1873. It was closed to regular passenger services in 1952. In 1977 Class 45 'Peak' No. 45015 passes through the closed station with a Toton to Tinsley service. (Phil Sangwell)

The station at Barrow Hill closed in 1954, although it continued to be used for special trains for some years. Nearby is the Barrow Hill engine shed, a roundhouse built around 1870 for the Staveley Iron & Coal Company. It became redundant in 1991 but the building was preserved and now houses the Barrow Hill Roundhouse and Railway Centre, which opened in 1998. On 6 October 1990 the shed is seen accommodating a number of Class 58 locomotives.

Killamarsh station originally opened in 1841, closed in 1843, and reopened in 1873. Killamarsh West, as it became under BR, closed to passengers in 1954. Three years later on 14 September 1957 Class 9F 2-10-0 No. 92108 heads north through the closed station with a Class H freight. (Ben Brooksbank)

The Birmingham & Derby Junction Railway

The Birmingham & Derby Junction Railway was authorised by an Act of 19 May 1836 to build a line from Derby to Hampton-in-Arden, on the London and Birmingham main line, and a branch to Curzon Street. Robert Stephenson was the engineer for the 42-mile line, which presented no great difficulties, and opened on 12 August 1839. There are just two of the line's stations in Derbyshire: Peartree and Willington. The latter has had various names since it opened with the railway in 1839. It closed as Repton and Willington in 1968 and reopened as Willington in 1994. On 27 February 1968, just a few weeks before closure, a Class 105 Cravens unit arrives at the station with the 16.20 Birmingham to Derby. (RCTS)

Pear Tree and Normanton station closed in March 1968 and reopened as Peartree in 1976. Just to the south of the station is Melbourne Junction. On 6 March 1966 the diverted 10.50 St Pancras to Manchester comes off the Chellaston branch at the junction. (RCTS)

The Midland Counties Railway

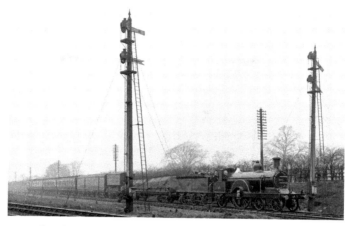

The original impetus for the Midland Counties Railway had been to enable the transport of coal from the mines of the Erewash Valley to Leicester. Later, extensions to Rugby and Nottingham were added to the plans and the Erewash Valley line dropped. These plans were authorised by an Act of 21 June 1836. Being the easiest to construct, work started on the line from Derby to Nottingham first and was completed by 4 June 1839. Trent Junction to Leicester followed on 5 May 1840, and Leicester to Rugby on 30 June the same year. There were originally three MCR stations in Derbyshire, at Breaston, Spondon, and Borrowash. Breaston later became Sawley and closed in 1930. Borrowash closed in 1966. Spondon remains open. Draycott was opened in 1852, renamed Draycott and Breaston in 1939 and closed in 1966. Sawley Junction opened in 1888. It was renamed Long Eaton in 1968 and remains open. It is the third station to bear the name. A theatrical train stands at Spondon Junction headed by Johnson '179' Class 1P 4-2-2 No. 665. These engines had driving wheels of 7 feet 6 inches. (Science Museum)

Derby

It was perhaps inevitable that Derby would become a major railway town given that it was the meeting place of the B&DJR, NMR, and the MCR. The railways sensibly agreed on a joint station that opened in 1840. There was a single long platform, as can be seen in this early print. Additional platforms were added later. Just four years later on 10 May 1844 the three railways amalgamated to form the Midland Railway.

An interior view of the station in around 1890. Clearly a quiet period, as there is a horse on the track!

During the Second World War the train shed was bombed and badly damaged. It was not repaired, but replaced in the early 1950s by individual concrete canopies. On 23 November 1981 Class 31 No. 31153 stands at the platform with a train of steel bar.

On the same date Class 46 'Peak' No. 46011 provides plenty of steam for the 12.18 Taunton to Newcastle. Notice the old station buildings and concrete canopy.

In 1985 the old railway buildings were demolished and a new entrance and booking hall completed. Between 2007 and 2009 the concrete canopies were all replaced. In 2018 the station trackwork was extensively remodelled and two new platforms created. On 5 March 2020 a Class 221 'Voyager' Cross Country unit stands under the new canopies with the 13.30 to Plymouth.

This is Railway Terrace, housing for the Midland Railway workers. These cottages are thought to be the earliest purpose-built accommodation in Britain for railway workers.

The Midland Hotel was designed by Francis Thompson and opened in 1842. It is a Grade II listed building.

The Midland Hotel was intended for the better class of person while people from the lower orders were expected to stay at The Brunswick Inn, situated at the other end of Railway Terrace.

The Railway Institute, built in 1894 as a recreational and cultural facility for railway employees. All these buildings, and the adjoining streets, are within the Midland Railway Conservation Area.

No. 1 Roundhouse was built by the North Midland Railway. It is the oldest railway roundhouse in the world and is listed Grade II*. Following years of dereliction, it was taken over and restored by Derby College.

The roundhouse interior in Victorian times.

On 2 April 1950 a line-up of engines at one of the later sheds. On the left is a 'Jubilee', together with three 'Black 5s'. At that time Derby had an allocation of 139 locomotives. (Ben Brooksbank)

Ten years later Johnson 3F 0-6-0 No. 43657 heads towards Trent with a coal train. In the background is No. 4 shed. (Ben Brooksbank)

A splendid panorama of the works taken from the station building. On the left is the former Midland Counties depot. In the centre is the familiar works clock tower with No. 1 Roundhouse behind. To the right is No. 2 Roundhouse and on the right is the station train shed.

A collection of Kirtley engines under construction in No. 8 Shop of the works.

The last locomotive to be repaired at Derby Works, Standard 4MT 4-6-0 No. 75042, outshopped on 20 Seeptember 1963.

In 1969 the works became part of British Rail Engineering Limited. In front of the works on 23 November 1981 stands Class 20 No. 20047.

At an open day on 16 September 1989 the sign has changed. That year the works was bought out by a group of private companies and employees.

The works offices in 2020, now part of Derby College. At some point a third storey was added to the building. Also, as part of the restoration, the right-hand upper storey has been rebuilt to match the rest of the building. It is listed Grade II*.

St Mary's Goods Depot pictured in 1989. On the left is the grain warehouse and on the right the Town Goods Shed. Both are listed Grade II, and happily both have now found new uses.

The New Line

The original North Midland route to Sheffield was via Rotherham. This route was taken to avoid 1 in 100 gradients in both directions south of Sheffield. The MR put this anomaly right by the opening of the 'New Road' from Tapton Junction to Sheffield in 1870. Thereafter the line via Rotherham became known as the 'Old Road'. On the New Road there were stations at Sheepbridge, Unstone, Dronfield, Dore and Totley, Beauchief, Millhouses, and Heeley. A new station, Pond Street, was built at Sheffield, later becoming known as Sheffield Midland. All the stations between Chesterfield and Sheffield, apart from Dore and Totley, closed between 1951 and 1968. Dronfield was temporarily reopened in February 1979 due to heavy snowfall causing traffic chaos in Sheffield. It was reopened permanently in 1981. In the 1980s Class 31 No. 31416 passes through the station with a Nottingham to Barrow-in-Furness train. (Phil Sangwell)

Dore and Totley station is seen at a date between 1894 when the route to Chinley (the lines seen curving to the left) was opened and 1902 when the lines from Sheffield were quadrupled. A pair of Johnson 4-4-0s head through with an Up express.

A colourised photograph of the station following quadrupling. The signal box has gone, to be replaced by a new one to the north of the station and the station has gained two new platforms and their accompanying buildings. In 1985 the curve from the New Road to the Chinley line was singled leaving Dore and Totley station with just one platform for both Up and Down services.

The Ecclesbourne Valley Railway

At one time it had been intended that construction of the EVR would continue through the Peak towards Manchester. However, once the MR had gained full control of the Manchester, Buxton, Matlock & Midlands Junction Railway this was no longer necessary. The 8½-mile line was authorised in 1863 and was opened to passengers on 1 October 1867. There were stations at Hazlewood, Shottle, Idridgehay and Wirksworth. The main traffics were limestone and milk. In 1895 there was a passenger service of four trains a day between Derby and Wirksworth with just one on Sundays. Passenger trains ceased in 1947 but the line continued to be used for freight, principally limestone. This traffic ended in 1991. This is a view of the yard at Wirksworth shortly after the cessation of this traffic. The yard is still owned by Network Rail and is listed as a Strategic Rail Site.

In 1996 Wyvern Rail were granted a Light Railway Order for the whole length of the line. Passenger trains started running on a short length of line in 2002, since when the railway has been slowly developed and now trains run from Duffield to Wirksworth. On 26 August 2020 Class 14 'Teddy Bear' No. D9537 arrives at Idridgehay with a Wirksworth–Duffield train. The 'Teddy Bears' had a very short working life on British Railways. Built in 1964/5, they were all withdrawn by 1970. The majority went on to have long working lives in British industry. No. D9537 worked at British Steel Corby before being preserved at the EVR.

The Erewash Valley Line

On 6 September 1847 the Erewash Valley line as far as Codnor Park was opened, creating a flat crossing with the Midland Counties line, known as Platt's Crossing. In 1862 Trent station opened to enable interchange between the two routes. At the same time a new north curve from Sawley Junction was built to give trains from Derby access to Trent's platforms, and Platt's crossing was removed. In 1869 the line from Stenson Junction joined the layout at Sheet Stores Junction. The freight lines from the Erewash Valley passing to the east of the station were opened in 1893, and elevated in 1901. Trent station was closed on 1 January 1968. Subsequently the north curve from Sawley Junction to Trent Station North Junction and the west to east curve joining the Erewash line to the Derby–Nottingham line were removed. At the south end of the station stands Johnson 2P 4-4-0 No. 387, as rebuilt by Richard Deeley.

Trent Station North Junction signal box. In the background can be seen the wide, island platform of the station. The gantry on the right carries signals as follows, reading left to right: Down main to Nottingham passenger, to Nottingham goods, to Toton passenger, and to Toton goods. Below the Nottingham line signals are Long Eaton Junction signal box's distant signals, and below the Toton line signals are North Erewash Junction signal box's distant signals.

Passing Trent station on the Up Slow on 24 April 1961 is Stanier 8F 2-8-0 No. 48355 with a train of empty ore wagons. The signal box is Trent Station South Junction. (Ben Brooksbank)

The Long Eaton station, seen here, dates from 1863. It was the second Long Eaton station on the Erewash Valley line. On 17 May 1962 BR-Sulzer Type 4 'Peak' No. D5 *Cross Fell* heads south through the station with a train of empty mineral wagons. D5 was one of the original series of ten locomotives with an engine rated at 2,300 hp, all named after English peaks. Long Eaton closed on 2 January 1967. (Ben Brooksbank)

Another station that closed on the same date is Stapleford and Sandiacre. Approaching the station on 17 May 1962 is Stanier 8F 2-8-0 No. 48641 with a southbound freight. (Ben Brooksbank)

On 20 June 1991 Class 58 No. 58104 passes through Stanton Gate sidings with a southbound MGR. These were sidings associated with the Stanton and Staveley Works, which closed in 2007.

Just north of Trowell Junction on 29 June 1991 Class 20s Nos 20071 and 20135 head the 10.38 Saturdays-only Skegness–Sheffield.

Passing in the opposite direction is a train of 'Seacow' hoppers headed by Class 20s Nos 20078 and 20163. Trowell station was located near the point where these photographs were taken. It opened on 2 June 1884 and was another January 1967 closure.

A service for Nottingham arrives at Ilkeston Junction. In the background is the GN Bennerley Viaduct. The wagons on the left are parked on the closed branch to Ilkeston Town. The station closed with the others on the line in January 1967, but a new Ilkeston station opened on the same site in 2017. (RCTS)

The Ilkeston branch opened in 1847 but Ilkeston station closed to passengers in 1870. It reopened on 1 July 1879 before finally closing to passengers in the late 1940s. The station is seen in LMS days.

At Langley Mill on 13 April 1960 Fowler 4F 0-6-0 No. 44321 passes with a train of empty wagons. This station also closed in 1967 but reopened in 1986. (Ben Brooksbank)

At Alfreton and Normanton station on 23 June 1961 4F 0-6-0 No. 44229 passes with a train of empties on the Down Fast. No. 44229 was built in 1926 and survived until November 1964. When withdrawn it was a Westhouses engine. (Ben Brooksbank)

Westhouses locomotive depot in 1983. The signal box is Blackwell East. (Dave Bevis)

An early twentieth-century view of Doe Hill station, which closed in 1960.

The Erewash Line Extension

The MR was authorised to extend its Erewash Valley line from Codnor Park to Mansfield in 1846. The Mansfield & Pinxton Railway had existed since 1819, connecting Mansfield with the Pinxton arm of the Cromford Canal. This line was taken over by the MR, which used the trackbed to build its own line, which opened on 9 October 1849. The station of Pinxton and Selston opened with the railway in 1848 and closed ninety-nine years later. Pinxton signal box closed in 2007 after 110 years' service. It has been preserved at Barrow Hill. Class 58 No. 58030 at the head of an empty MGR train sets off after a signal check. Note that fixed to the Up starter signal (on the left) is a colour light signal. This is the Sleights East distant, which shows amber when the Pinxton home is pulled off and green when Sleights home is pulled off. The photograph was taken on 27 July 1991.

The extension into the Leen Valley was further extended from Mansfield to Worksop in June 1875, where it connected with the MS&L line from Sheffield to Lincoln. North of Mansfield was Shirebrook Colliery. This is a view of Shirebrook Colliery and Sidings in 1992. The colliery had closed the previous year. Shirebrook Sidings signal box was destroyed by fire in 1971. The replacement box is the small white structure that can be seen beyond the signal. Nothing remains here now except the Up and Down Mansfield lines.

Shirebrook TMD opened in June 1965. The work of the locomotives stabled here was primarily concerned with the movement of coal to power stations. Declining traffic led to its closure in 1996. Shirebrook station signal box closed the following year. In the background is the former Shirebrook West station. This closed in October 1964 but was reopened in 1998 as Shirebrook, one of the stations on the Robin Hood line. The photograph was taken on 20 April 1991.

Shirebrook Junction. The line to the right is the Lancashire, Derbyshire & East Coast Railway line to Lincoln. The line on the left leads to W. H. Davis wagon works. The locomotive passing the signal box on 17 February 1992 is Class 56 No. 56016.

Heading south through Elmton and Creswell Junction on 13 March 1993 is Class 56 No. 56003 with an empty MGR train. The branch line passing behind the signal box led to Seymour Junction. This is another location that has gained a railway station.

Whitwell station closed in October 1964. In 1981 the station buildings were dismantled and rebuilt at Butterley. A new station on the original site was opened in May 1998. On 20 April 1991 a Class 58 heads north with a loaded MGR.

Between Derwent and Erewash

The line from Little Eaton Junction to Ripley opened on 1 September 1856. Its main purpose was to serve the collieries at Denby and Marehay. There were stations at Little Eaton, Coxbench, Kilburn, Denby and Ripley. This line largely superseded the Little Eaton Gangway, a 4-foot 6-inch plateway that paralleled the new line between Denby and Little Eaton. This had been opened by Benjamin Outram in 1795 to connect the collieries to the Derby Canal. The tramway continued in use until 1908, when this photograph was taken.

Coxbench station closed to passengers in June 1930 and to freight on 5 August 1957. In 1895 there was a service of just four trains daily between Derby and Ripley.

Denby was originally Smithy Houses. It shortly became Deneby, and in 1878 Denby. It closed to passengers in June 1930, along with the other stations on the line, and to freight in 1965. On 17 October 1965 the LCGB Derbyshire Railtour visited the branch. Class 4F 0-6-0 No. 44113 is seen propelling the train through Denby towards Marehay Crossing. (RCTS)

The branch remained open for coal traffic. On 7 July 1993 Class 56 No. 56018 is seen at Little Eaton Crossing with a loaded MGR from Denby Colliery.

The line from Ambergate to Pye Bridge opened in 1875. Intended mainly as a through route for freight there was just one intermediate station, at Butterley. Passenger services were withdrawn on 16 June 1947 and freight on 23 December 1968. Today the station enjoys a new lease of life on the preserved Midland Railway. On 30 August 1993 Princess Royal 4-6-2 No. 46203 *Princess Margaret Rose* is seen at Butterley station. (Ben Brooksbank)

The line from Butterley through Ripley to Heanor was opened on 2 June 1890. A new station was opened at Ripley and the old station used as a goods depot. A Sentinel steam railcar was tried in the 1920s but it didn't stop the station closing to passengers in 1930. Goods and excursion traffic continued until 1963. The line between Ripley and Butterley closed in 1938.

Left: A view south at Ripley Junction in 1926. This is where the two single-track lines to Little Eaton and to Heanor diverged.

Below: Crosshill and Codnor, the only other station on this line, in around 1904. It was closed temporarily between 1917 and 1920 and then permanently in 1926. In 1929 the track between Ripley and Heanor was lifted.

Heanor station opened on 2 June 1890. It was to be another five years before the line was completed to Heanor Junction on the Erewash Valley line. A branch was also built to a second Langley Mill station, which closed in 1926. Like Crosshill and Codnor, Heanor closed temporarily in 1917 and permanently in 1926. It remained open for goods traffic until 1951, by which time it had become Heanor North.

Through the Peak

The Manchester, Buxton, Matlock & Midlands Junction Railway had grand plans but unfortunately not the money to match. Its line from Ambergate to Rowsley, completed in 1849, was as far as it got. Both the Midland and the Manchester & Birmingham had an interest in the line and in 1852 agreed to jointly lease the MBM&MJR. It would be worked by the Midland. The Stockport, Disley & Whaley Bridge Railway was building towards Buxton and in 1860 the MR obtained an Act to build the 15-mile line from Rowsley to meet the SD&WBR at Buxton. The line reached Hassop in 1862 and Buxton in 1863. On 23 June 1961 Stanier 8F 2-8-0 No. 48547 heads a short Up freight through Whatstandwell station. The first station at this location was to the north of the tunnel seen in the background and was known as Whatstandwell Bridge. The present station was opened in 1894.

A superb photo of Midland 4-4-0 compound No. 1021 passing through Cromford with an Up express in 1911. No. 1021 is one of the original Deeley compounds with 7-foot driving wheels. A further 195 compounds were built by the LMS with 6-foot 9-inch drivers.

Over a hundred years later, on 5 March 2020, unit No. 156916 arrives with a service for Newark Castle. Comparison with the earlier photo shows that the buildings have not changed at all. The building on the Up platform is the original station building, thought to have been designed by G. H. Stokes. The buildings on the Down platform were added later by the MR. All the buildings are listed Grade II.

At Matlock, the present terminus of the line from Ambergate, on 21 June 1969, just one year after the closure of the line to the north, a Class 104 unit has arrived with a service from Derby. (J.W. Sutherland)

This is the original terminus of the MBM&MJR at Rowsley. When the MR extended the line to Buxton a new station was built and the old station became a goods office. It is seen here in 1989. Subsequently the Joseph Paxton-designed, Grade II listed building has been refurbished and is now a shopping outlet.

Class 45 'Peak' No. D90 was just three months old when this photo was taken on 23 June 1961. It is hauling train 1H13, the 10.25 St Pancras to Manchester Central through Bakewell, due in Manchester at 2.37 p.m. D90 had a short working life, being withdrawn as No. 45008 in 1980. (Ben Brooksbank)

On the same date, further north at Hassop, we see ex-LMS 4F 0-6-0 No. 44038 drifting down the 1 in 100 gradient near Hassop with an Up coal empties. The LMS 4F 0-6-0 was a Midland design dating back to 1911. Construction of these engines continued for many years after the Grouping, the last being completed in 1941. (Ben Brooksbank)

Great Longstone for Ashford station was situated on the road between those two places, and not particularly near either. In 1960 just four trains a day on weekdays stopped here, and none on Sundays. Perhaps unsurprisingly it closed just two years later.

At Monsal Head the railway enters the Wye Valley and the most heavily engineered part of the route. Between Monsal Head and Peak Forest there are two major viaducts and six tunnels, and a final climb at 1 in 90 to reach the summit of the line. The importance of Miller's Dale was as an interchange station for Buxton trains, rather than providing a service for the local population, of which there was little. The 1953 timetable shows a shuttle service between the two stations with one London train per day attaching/detaching carriages from Buxton. On 3 June 1966 Park Royal railbus No. M79973, seen here at Miller's Dale, was in charge of the service. Reliability issues led to its replacement the same year and scrapping the following year. (J.W. Sutherland)

At Buxton, the Midland and LNW stations were next door to each other, designed in an identical style by Joseph Paxton. On 25 February 1967 a Derby Lightweight unit stands in the Midland station with the Miller's Dale shuttle. (The Jeyes)

Miller's Dale to New Mills

Frustrated in its attempts to reach Manchester, the MR came to an agreement with the MS&L that would give it access to the MS&L. The MS&L built the line from Hyde to New Mills, together with the branch to Hayfield, while the Midland extended their line from Miller's Dale to New Mills via Chinley. The Marple, New Mills & Hayfield Junction Railway opened on 1 July 1865. Strines station followed in 1866 and Hayfield in 1868. The Midland's line opened in 1867. In 1869 the MNM&HJR was absorbed jointly by the MSL and MR and from 1872 was administered by the Sheffield and Midland Railways Joint Committee. In 1967 a Manchester Central to St Pancras train heads through Miller's Dale Junction. The line to the left leads to Buxton. (RCTS)

Although the line from Matlock to Peak Forest Junction closed, the line from Buxton via Peak Forest Junction to Chinley remained open for freight, principally for the transport of limestone from the various quarries in the area. On 14 April 1993 at Great Rocks Junction Class 37 No. 37688 sets back into Tunstead Siding with returning empties from Hindlow.

Despite their diminutive size, the Class 25s were the most common traction on the Tunstead to ICI Northwich trains in the early 1980s. Class 25 No. 25106 blasts its way up the 1 in 90 with banking assistance in the rear.

Also frequently seen in that period were Class 40s. One of the later series of split headcode engines whistles its way up the incline.

Much less common were Class 45s. On this occasion Class 45 No .45003 is tackling the climb. At the rear is a Class 40.

From the early 1990s Class 60s started to be used on the various workings through Peak Forest. On 1 May 1999 Pioneer Class 60 No. 60001 *Steadfast* heads through Chinley South Junction with the returning train 6H55 from Bletchley.

The importance of Chinley station at the turn of the twentieth century can be judged by its five platforms and bay. It was the meeting point of the Millers Dale and Hope Valley lines and was an important interchange station. There was also considerable detaching and attaching of train portions.

In 1981 Class 40 No. 40079 rumbles down the 1 in 90 through a much diminished Chinley station with a load of limestone for ICI.

In the early 1980s Class 31s plus Mark 2 sets were introduced on the South Trans-Pennine route to replace the Class 123/124 multiple units. On 6 April 1988 Class 31 No. 31221 heads the 13.45 Liverpool to Sheffield through New Mills South Junction. In the background a Hope Valley stopping service waits for the road.

A short time later Class 37s Nos 37676 and 37686, in the short-lived Railfreight 'red stripe' livery, thread their way through the pointwork with empty wagons for Peak Forest. In the left background is Newtown Viaduct, which carries the line leading to Hazel Grove and Cheadle. This line was constructed in 1902, giving the MR a more direct route to Manchester Central.

The Cheadle line, as well as being used by the South Trans-Pennine services, is also an important freight artery. On 26 May 1998 Class 56 No. 56073, wearing Transrail livery, heads train 6H34 Widnes to Earles Sidings away from the 3,866-yard-long Disley Tunnel.

A view taken of Hayfield station in September 1966 gives a good chance to compare old and new liveries. There can be little doubt about which is the more elegant. In 1960 Strines, New Mills and Hayfield had an hourly service, enhanced in the morning and evening peaks. On Sundays there were no fewer than fifteen trains to and from Hayfield, a service due in some part to the popularity of Hayfield as a starting point for ramblers heading for the Peak. The Hayfield branch closed in 1970. (Geoffrey Skelsey)

On 5 March 1982 a Class 108 waits to depart from New Mills Central with a service for Manchester Piccadilly.

The Midland in North-East Derbyshire

The railway from Westhouses to Teversall opened on 1 May 1886. It was extended to Pleasley in April 1877 and through to Mansfield Woodhouse on 1 May 1886. The line left the Trent–Clay Cross main line at Tibshelf and Blackwell Junction, the route being taken by the pair of Class 20s in this photograph. In the background is the branch to Blackwell Colliery. Nos 20173 and 20189 were photographed in July 1978. (Martin Addison)

Seymour Junction to Elmton and Cresswell opened in 1888. Clowne and Barlborough was the one intermediate station. The station went through various name changes during its lifetime before it finally closed to passengers on 5 July 1954. In its last year it had just one train daily, mainly for the benefit of schoolchildren, running between Chesterfield and Elmton and Cresswell, extended to Shirebrook West in term time. On summer Saturdays there was a through train to Blackpool and these trains continued until 1962. Although the rails have been lifted, the trackbed between Seymour Junction and Oxcroft has been protected for possible future use. Class 56 No. 56074 passes through the closed station with an empty MGR. (Phil Sangwell)

The Doe Lea line from Seymour Junction to Pleasley opened over a period of twenty-seven years. First came the section between Seymour Junction and Bolsover Woodhouse in May 1866, followed by the extension to Glapwell twenty years later. Finally the line to Pleasley was opened on 1 September 1890. There were several coal mines along its length, including Markham, the largest coal mine in North Derbyshire. Class 47 No. 47278 heads out of the colliery with an MGR. In the background the chimneys of Bolsover Coalite works can be seen. Markham closed in July 1993. (Phil Sangwell)

The Coalite works opened in 1937. It is seen here in full production in 1992. It subsequently fell foul of the financial difficulties of its owning company and ceased production.

A view of the closed Bolsover station looking south, taken on 13 July 1963. Other stations were Palterton and Sutton, Glapwell, and Rowthorn and Hardwick. The line lost its passenger service in 1930 but excursion trains from Bolsover continued to run until 1981. The line from Seymour Junction to Bolsover has been mothballed for possible future use. (Ben Brooksbank)

South Derbyshire

The Leicester & Swannington Railway opened in 1833. Later, now part of the MR, the line was extended to Leicester Junction, just south of Burton-on-Trent. Branches to Swadlincote and Wooden Box (Woodville from 1868) were opened in 1851 to serve the many collieries and other industries in the area. A line to join these two branches and complete the Swadlincote Loop was finished in 1883. Passenger services on the Loop ended in 1947 and freight in 1964. Passenger services on the Leicester Burton line ended on 7 September 1964. The line remains open for freight. There have been a number of plans to reopen the line to passengers but thus far none has made any progress. Hughes-Fowler 'Crab' 2-6-0 No. 42756 is seen at Woodville station with the SLS Leicestershire Railtour on 4 September 1962. (J.W. Sutherland)

A branch was authorised from Pear Tree on the B&DJ line to Ashby-de-la-Zouch in 1864/5. The section from Pear Tree (Melbourne Junction) to Melbourne was opened on 1 September 1868 and through to Ashby on 1 January 1874. There were stations at Chellaston and Swarkestone, Melbourne, Tonge and Breedon, Worthington, and Ashby. Melbourne station is seen in Midland Railway days.

Another branch, from Trent to Weston-on-Trent, was opened on 6 December 1869 and extended to Stenson Junction on the B&DJ on 3 November 1873. There were stations at Castle Donington and Shardlow, and Weston. The section common to both lines was between Chellaston West Junction and Chellaston East Junction. Both lines lost their passenger service on 22 September 1930. The Ashby line closed completely in 1980 but the Sheet Stores to Stenson line remains open for freight. A special train from the Stenson Junction direction passes Chellaston West signal box, hauled by a Caprotti 'Black 5' 4-6-0.

At Weston-on-Trent on 31 December 1967, Class 4 'Peak' hauls train 1H46, the diverted 08.45 Sundays St Pancras to Manchester. (RCTS)

On 7 July 1995 Class 60 No. 60076 *Suilven* passes along the Sheet Stores–Stenson line with a loaded MGR.

The Hope Valley

Above: There had been discussions about building a railway through the Hope Valley since the 1830s, with the aim of connecting Manchester and Sheffield. Unsurprisingly nothing came of these plans when faced with the problem of overcoming the hills at either end of the valley. In fact the railway traverses two valleys: the Vale of Edale and the Hope Valley. At the eastern end of the former land rises to more than 1,200 feet and at the western end of the latter to more than 1,700 feet. The Dore & Chinley Railway was authorised in 1884 but, unable to make sufficient progress, was absorbed by the MR in 1888. The 20-mile eight-chains line includes two of the longest tunnels in Britain – the 3,727-yard Cowburn Tunnel and the 6,226-yard Totley Tunnel. It finally opened to goods traffic in November 1893 and to regular passenger traffic on 1 June 1884. There were stations at Grindleford, Hathersage, Bamford, Hope, and Edale, all of which remain open. Work at Grindleford is nearing conclusion. Totley Tunnel is beyond the bridge.

Left: February 2003 saw the return, if only briefly, of St Pancras–Manchester services, due to the Stockport blockade. On 16 February an HST forming the 10.00 St Pancras to Manchester passes Grindleford signal box.

At Hathersage on 26 September 1966 Brush Type 2 (later Class 31) No. D5578 arrives with the 16.30 Sheffield to Chinley. (J.W. Sutherland)

Hope station shortly after opening. In 1895 nine trains called at Hope, although three of these only did so if requested. There were three services on Sundays.

A similar view taken in 1980 as a New Mills–Sheffield service arrives. The footbridge has survived but nothing else has. By 1960 Hope had twelve services on weekdays and six on Sundays. One of these was from Sheffield only as far as Hope in the morning, with a return working in the evening. Clearly a service designed for ramblers.

Earle's cement works was established in 1929 and has always been an important customer of the railways. A 1½-mile branch leads to the factory. Earles, now part of Lafarge, has its own locomotives which trip the wagons to the exchange sidings. On 21 April 1981 Class 40 No. 40139 pulls out of the sidings and heads west with a rake of 'Presflo' cement wagons.

The Hope Valley line was listed for closure in the Beeching Report while neither the Woodhead nor the Miller's Dale routes were. Its survival may be due to the presence of this important customer for rail. In the early 2000s it was producing 1.5 million tons of cement annually, nearly all of which was moved by rail. Inwards are the flows of limestone, fuel and other materials. On 26 May 1981 a pair of Class 105 Cravens units pass Earles Sidings with the 16.25 Hull to Manchester Piccadilly.

On 15 October 1981 the Class 123/4 unit forming the 11.20 Sheffield to Manchester Piccadilly has been brought to a stand by the signalman at Earles box to be warned of sheep on the line.

A little later Class 46 'Peak' No. 46016, having also been stopped, gets under way again with the 07.17 Harwich Parkeston Quay to Manchester Piccadilly 'Boat Train'.

Passing Edale signal box on 31 August 1992 is Class 158 No. 158782 with the 08.54 Liverpool to Norwich.

Climbing the 1 in 100 to Cowburn Tunnel on 11 April 1981 is Class 45 'Peak' No. 45065 with a special working.

The London & North Western Railway

The Cromford & High Peak Railway

The CHPR ran from the Cromford Canal to the Peak Forest Canal at Whaley Bridge. The Act was passed on 2 May 1825. The 15½ miles from Cromford Wharf to Hindlow opened on 29 May 1830 and the remaining 17½ miles from Hurdlow to Whaley Bridge on 1 July 1831. The profile of the CHPR was extraordinary. The central, adhesion-worked section of about 27 miles was on a plateau. At either end of the line were inclines worked by stationary engines; nine of these in all. Later changes reduced this number to seven. The plateau section of the line was worked by horses until 1833 when the first locomotive was delivered. The bottom of the Middleton incline is seen on the occasion of a railtour on 22 April 1961. The locomotive at the far end of the train is ex-LMS 0-4-0ST No. 47007. (J.W. Sutherland)

In 1853 the line at the Cromford end was extended to the Manchester, Buxton, Matlock & Midland Junction Railway at High Peak Junction and in 1857 at the Whaley Bridge end to the Stockport, Disley, & Whaley Bridge Railway. In 1862 the railway was leased to the LNWR and in 1887 the two companies amalgamated. The LNWR carried out major changes to the route. These included the abandonment of the line between Ladmanlow and Whaley Bridge and the construction of a new line from Hindlow to Buxton, which was ready by 1892. This is the line that is still in use today. The line between Parsley Hay and Hindlow was doubled and realigned and a new line was built between Parsley Hay and Ashbourne, opening on 4 August 1899. On 29 March 1949 a mineral train has just ascended the 1 in 8.5 Sheep Pasture incline headed by ex-LNW Webb Class 1P 2-4-0T No. 26428. The building on the right is the locomotive shed and just seen beyond that is the engine house. (Walter Dendy)

Middleton Top with the locomotive shed and engineman's cottage and engine house behind. The 1829 Butterley engine at Middleton Top has been restored and can be seen working on certain days of the year. (Walter Dendy)

Ex-North London
Railway 0-6-0T
No. 58856 shunts
wagons at Middleton
Top, *c.* 1953.

The infamous Gotham
Curve, with a radius of
just 55 yards. In 1964
an RCTS tour makes its
way round the curve at
the maximum speed of
5 mph.

On 21 August 1964, at
Friden, ex-LNER J94
0-6-0ST No. 68102
stands with a pair of
water tenders. This
locomotive, along with
many others, was built
by Hunslet for the
War Department and
later purchased by the
LNER. It was withdrawn
with the closure of
the CHPR in 1967.
(J.W. Sutherland)

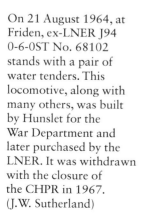

The transhipment warehouse at Whaley Bridge where freight was transferred to the Peak Forest Canal. The original building dates from 1801 but has since been much modified. It is listed Grade ll*. (J.W. Sutherland)

A variety of locomotives worked on the line during its lifetime. In LNW days these included the 'Crewe Goods' 2-4-0 and 2-4-0T, to be replaced later by Webb 4-foot 8.5-inch 2-4-0Ts. In 1931 a number of North London Railway 0-6-0 tanks arrived. Other engines included ex-MR 0-6-0T, ex-LNW 0-8-0, 4F 0-6-0, 8F 2-8-0, J94 0-6-0T, and various ex-LMS 2-6-4T. LNW 2-4-0T No. 3049 is seen near the top of Hopton incline.

The Buxton Line

The Stockport & Whaley Bridge Railway Act was passed on 31 July 1854. The aim of the railway was to connect with the Cromford & High Peak, and a further Act was passed to enable an extension from Whaley Bridge to the C&HP. The line was completed by 28 May 1857, public services starting on 6 June, worked from the outset by the LNW. There were stations at Hazel Grove, Disley, New Town (New Mills), Furness Vale and Whaley Bridge. A number of other stations opened subsequently: Davenport in 1858, Middlewood in 1879, and Woodsmoor in 1990. An Act for the extension to Buxton was passed on 27 July 1857. The extension was opened to public services on 15 June 1863. Intermediate stations were at Chapel-en-le-Frith and Dove Holes. There were some steep gradients on the line. After Whaley Bridge the line rose at 1 in 60/58 for 7 miles, before falling at 1 in 66 to Buxton. On 14 June 1958 a Class 104 unit arrives at New Mills Newtown with the 4.15 p.m. Buxton to Manchester London Road. (J.W. Sutherland)

In 1895 the line saw sixteen services on weekdays. Eight of these were to Buxton, four to Hazel Grove, one to Disley and one to Whaley Bridge. Two trains continued to Parsley Hay. The fastest train between Manchester and Buxton took one hour five minutes. There were additional services on Saturdays but only two trains on Sundays. At Furness Vale on 22 May 1959 a Stanier 4MT 2-6-4 arrives with a Manchester to Buxton service. (J.W. Sutherland)

Ex-LNW 7F 0-8-0 No. 49191 shunts the yard at New Mills Newtown in September 1959. (J.W. Sutherland)

The fireman puts the bag in at Whaley Bridge on 18 October 1958. Notice that ex-LNW 7F No. 49428 is equipped with a tender cab, fairly essential when working up to Buxton at 1,000 feet above sea level. (J.W. Sutherland)

At Bibbington's Sidings on 23 May 1959 Stanier 8F 2-8-0 No. 48246 takes a freight working to Hooton on to the Down Slow line. The other locomotive is Johnson 3F 0-6-0 No. 43562, which has just banked the train up the 1 in 60 gradient from Buxton. (J.W. Sutherland)

At Buxton on 24 April 1953 Fowler 4MT 2-6-4 No. 42371 stands ready to leave with the 9.05 a.m. to Manchester London Road. Notice the gradient post showing 1 in 135. This will shortly steepen to 1 in 60. In 1953 there were sixteen or seventeen services on weekdays, two or three of these to and from Whaley Bridge or Disley. In the evening peak seven trains left Manchester between 4.45 and 5.50 p.m., the fastest of these taking fifty minutes to Buxton. In the Down direction the 8.20 a.m. from Buxton called only at Stockport and reached Manchester London Road at 9.01 a.m. (J.W. Sutherland)

Many years later services are in the hands of Class 150 DMUs. On 2 May 1998 unit No. 150144 approaches the station with a service from Manchester Piccadilly. In 2020 there is a basic half-hourly service between Manchester and Hazel Grove, and hourly between Manchester and Buxton, half-hourly in the peaks. Fastest Up journey time is fifty-four minutes, and forty-eight in the Down direction.

On 16 July 1998 Mainline-liveried Class 60 No. 60044 waits to leave the yard with train 6P56, a Dowlow to Ashburys working. No. 60044 was one of the few locomotives to receive the full Mainline livery by the short-lived, eponymous freight company.

The Class 104 diesel multiple units were introduced to the Buxton line in 1957 and were always strongly associated with that line. The units were withdrawn on 6 May 1989 and specially prepared unit No. N669 can be seen approaching Stockport station on the last day of service with the 13.08 Manchester Piccadilly to Buxton.

The Ashbourne Line

The Act for the railway from Ashbourne to Buxton was passed on 4 August 1892. The only new section of railway was from Parsley Hay to Ashbourne and was completed by 1899. The line was single track throughout, with passing places at all stations except Thorpe Cloud. The line was never developed as a major route despite at one time seeing through coaches between Euston and Buxton. In 1953, the last full year of passenger services, the line saw just four trains daily between Buxton and Uttoxeter in the Up direction. The two afternoon trains did not run on Saturdays. In the Down direction there were two trains throughout, two between Uttoxeter and Ashbourne, and one between Ashbourne and Buxton. Passenger services ended on 30 October the following year. The line closed progressively to freight, closing altogether in 1967. At Higher Buxton in June 1930 Webb 1P 0-6-2T No. 6899 stands with a service for Uttoxeter.

Buxton's ex-LNW 7F 0-8-0 No. 49439 is seen shunting at Hindlow on 4 May 1962. No. 49439 was withdrawn at the end of the year. (J.W. Sutherland)

On 14 April 1993 Class 37 No. 37688 emerges from Hindlow Tunnel into a lunar landscape with a Hindlow to Tunstead empties working.

At Parsley Hay No. 49439 is seen again with a train for Pinfold Sidings, Uttoxeter. (J.W. Sutherland)

A view of the junction between the CHPR and Ashbourne lines just south of Parsley Hay on 15 May 1956. The train hauled by Fowler 4MT 2-6-4T No. 42350 and Stanier 2-6-4T No. 42658 is an excursion from Manchester to Ashbourne for the well dressing. (J.W. Sutherland)

At Hartington on 4 September 1962 Edgeley's Fowler 4MT No. 42343 is seen with the Stephenson Locomotive Society Leicestershire Railtour. (J.W. Sutherland)

Alsop-en-le-Dale on 4 May 1962 sees the meeting of two ex-LNW 7F 0-8-0s. No. 49439 stands in the station with a working for Pinfold Sidings as No. 49281 arrives with a Uttoxeter to Buxton working. The car is a Ford Popular 103E, equipped with a three-speed gearbox. In 1962 one of these could be bought for £395. (J.W. Sutherland)

In 1948 Fowler 2-6-4T No. 42371 stands at Tissington with a service for Buxton. (Phil Sangwell)

Thorpe Cloud for Dovedale was the only station on the line that did not have a passing loop. Thorpe Cloud is the name of a hill at the entry to Dovedale. (J.W. Sutherland)

The opening of the Buxton–Ashbourne line saw the building of a new joint station at Ashbourne further to the north of the previous one. Thompson B1 4-6-0 No. 61004 *Oryx* is at the head of an RCTS railtour of the Midlands on 11 May 1963. No. 61004 was named after a species of antelope, like a number of others of the same class, including No. 61005 *Bongo*. As a result the whole class was known colloquially as 'Bongos'. (Ben Brooksbank)

No trace now remains of the station buildings at Ashbourne but the rather splendid goods shed survives and is seen in 1995.

Clifton station opened when the North Staffordshire Railway completed its branch from Rocester, on the Churnet Valley line, to Ashbourne in 1852. In 1958 Fowler 4MT 2-6-4T approaches the station with a freight for Pinfold Sidings. (J.W. Sutherland)

The Great Central Railway

The Woodhead Line

The Woodhead Line from Manchester to Sheffield was a project of the Sheffield, Ashton-under-Lyne & Manchester Railway. The company was incorporated by an Act of 5 May 1837. Construction of the Woodhead Tunnel, the major engineering feature of the line, started in October 1838. In the meantime the line was built out from Manchester, reaching Dinting (originally named Glossop) on 24 December 1842. The line was extended to Hadfield and Woodhead by 1844. The 3-mile 22-yard tunnel was completed in 1845, the official opening of the line taking place on the 22 December. A second bore was completed in 1853. This view dates from August 1953 and the new tunnel, on the right, is still under construction. K3 2-6-0 No. 61852 emerges from the Down tunnel at Woodhead with a mixed freight. (Ben Brooksbank)

In the mid-1930s the LNER drew up plans to electrify the line at 1500 V dc. Work started but was held up by the Second World War. In 1948 work, which included the building of a new double-bore tunnel, was resumed and the new electric railway opened in 1954. In 1970 passenger services were withdrawn and in 1981 the line was closed completely west of the tunnel except for the section to Hadfield and the branch to Glossop. In 1984 these lines were converted to 25kV ac and the Class 506 EMUs withdrawn. In July 1977 this Class 506 EMU, having called at Glossop, is passing through Dinting en route to Hadfield. It will return to Dinting on its way to Manchester. (Eastbank Model Railway Club)

In the 1960s a Class 76 crosses Dinting Viaduct with a service for Sheffield. In 1960 there were eighteen services daily between Manchester and Sheffield, with eleven on Sundays. There were originally two stations between Hadfield and the tunnel: Crowden, closed in 1957, and Woodhead, closed in 1964. In 1960 Woodhead had an extremely sparse service. Just one service per day in each direction, with an additional service on Wednesday, Thursday, Friday and Saturday. (RCTS)

On 26 August 2020 a Class 323 unit arrives at Dinting from Hadfield en route to Manchester.

The third side of the layout at Dinting, not normally used. The usual calling pattern is Dinting, Hadfield, Glossop, Hadfield, Dinting, then to Manchester.

Hadfield in July 1977 when it was still a station on a through route. (Eastbank Model Railway Club)

A photograph taken from the same vantage point in 2020. Hard to believe it is the same place.

The line from Dinting to Glossop was built at his own expense by the Duke of Norfolk and later sold to the SA&M. It opened in June 1845. This is the station exterior. Notice the lion, a symbol of the Norfolk family.

A pair of Class 76s pass through the closed Woodhead station with an empty MGR on 18 April 1981, exactly three months before closure of the line to all traffic.

The Derbyshire Lines

In the 1880s the MS&L aspired to reach Chesterfield and to access the North Midland Coalfield. Its first attempt was thwarted by Parliament but if finally obtained its Act in 1889. This Act provided for a line from Woodhouse Junction to Annesley, where it would connect with the Great Northern's Leen Valley line, and a branch from Staveley to Chesterfield. A further Act provided for a line from Chesterfield southwards, regaining the Annesley line at Heath. This become known as the Chesterfield Loop. These lines were collectively known as the MS&L/GC Derbyshire Lines. Beighton to Staveley opened on 1 June 1892 and the branch to Chesterfield a few days later the line through to Anneseley was opened on 2 January 1893, and the loop to Heath on 3 July the same year. These new lines not only gave access to the Nottinghamshire collieries but also provided a route to London via the GNR system. On 23 August 1963 Class O1 2-8-0 (rebuild of GC Class O4) No. 63786 passes southbound through Killamarsh Central with iron ore empties. There were eventually three stations at Killamarsh. Now there are none. (Ben Brooksbank)

There were two stations called Eckington and Renishaw. Needless to say neither has survived. The GC station became Renishaw Central in 1950. The Derbyshire lines lost their passenger service on 4 March 1963. This is a view southwards at the GC station.

Almost inevitably there were two Staveley Town stations. From 1950 the GC station became known as Staveley Central. This a view from Staveley Central South Junction taken in the mid-1960s. The line curving away to the right is to Chesterfield Central. In the left background is the closed GC Staveley shed. The train is a Bournemouth to York service. (RCTS)

Parker Ex-GC N4 0-6-2 No. 5637 stands at Staveley shed. This type, introduced in 1889, worked almost exclusively in the Sheffield area handling steelworks and colliery traffic and shunting in marshalling yards. No. 5637 was allocated BR number 69241 but never carried it. It was withdrawn in 1949.

Pilsley was built in a similar style to Eckington and other stations on the line. It closed completely on 2 November 1959. There were no stations between Staveley and Heath on the 'main line', so that passenger services between Sheffield Victoria and Nottingham ran via the Chesterfield Loop. In 1895 Pilsley enjoyed a service of six trains in each direction on weekdays. The timetable for the whole line was extremely complicated, with trains from Sheffield terminating at one of six different stations. There were also variations according to the day of the week.

The Lancashire, Derbyshire & East Coast Railway

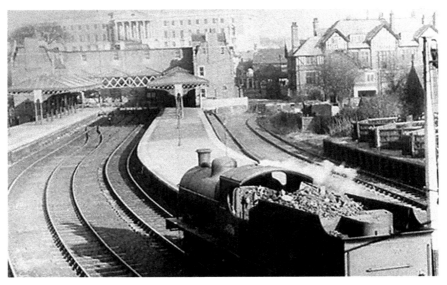

The LD&ECR originally envisaged a network of some 170 miles, stretching from Warrington in the west to Sutton-on-Sea in the east. The main purpose of the railway would be the movement of coal west to the industrial north-west and east for export at a new harbour to be built at Sutton. The company received its Act on 5 August 1891 authorising the construction of a line from Chesterfield to Pyewipe Junction, Lincoln. Barlborough Colliery to Pyewipe Junction opened in November 1896 and the remainder of the line in March 1897. The terminus in Chesterfield was at Chesterfield Market Place, seen here in the 1950s. The locomotive is a Robinson J11 0-6-0, a design introduced at the turn of the century.

Horns Bridge, Chesterfield. The lowest level line is the GC line from Central station; above that the Midland main line, and at the highest level the LD&ECR.

Although built primarily as line for the transport of coal, a passenger service was also provided. There were six trains daily between Chesterfield and Langwith Junction and three from there to Lincoln. By 1947 the service had changed little. At that time the 39½-mile journey between Lincoln and Chesterfield took one hour forty-five minutes. On summer Saturdays there was a through service from Market Place to Skegness, leaving at 7.55 a.m. and arriving at 11.09 a.m. At Arkwright Town Robinson A5/1 4-6-2 No.69815 stands with a Lincoln–Chesterfield service. The passenger service between Chesterfield and Shirebrook North ceased on 3 December 1951.

Bolsover in LD&ECR days. The station was renamed Bolsover South in 1950.

At Scarcliffe in 1911 the station master poses with his family. The station master was probably little troubled with business from the village, whose population was at that time numbered in hundreds.

Langwith Junction was the location where the LD&ECR Beighton branch joined. The company had ambitions to reach Sheffield. A line from Barlborough Junction, just west of Clowne, was completed to Beighton Junction by May 1900. From there to Treeton Junction the LD&ECR ran over MR metals and again from Brightside to Sheffield Midland. In this view looking north at Langwith the lifted line to Clowne and Beighton is seen on the left. (RCTS)

A view south from the same point shows the Leen Valley line curving away to the right. (RCTS)

The GNR's Leen Valley line reached Langwith Junction in 1901. In January 1907 the LD&ECR was purchased by the Great Central, which itself became part of the LNER in 1923, after which the station was renamed Shirebrook North. On 26 March 1966 B1 4-6-0 No. 61302 stands in the station with the RCTS Eight Counties Railtour. (Ben Brooksbank)

At Upperthorpe and Killamarsh another stationmaster poses with his family. Passenger services between Shirebrook North and Sheffield ceased on 11 September 1939.

The Great Northern Railway

The GNR had long been frustrated in their attempts to gain access to the lucrative coal traffic emanating from the Erewash Valley. The company brought forward a plan for a line from Colwick curving north round Nottingham as far as Awsworth Junction, to the west of Kimberley, where a branch would head up the valley to Codnor Park and Pinxton. The main line would continue west through Ilkeston and Derby to reach the North Staffordshire Railway at Egginton Junction. Authorisation was received on 25 July 1872 and the line to Pinxton was opened on 23 August 1875, initially for coal traffic. Passenger trains started running on 1 August the following year. The line from Awsworth Junction opened to freight traffic from 28 January 1878 and to passengers on 1 April. Between Awsworth and Ilkeston is the magnificent Bennerley Viaduct. A quarter of a mile long and constructed of wrought iron, it is a Grade II* listed structure.

Ilkeston station is seen at the turn of the century. It became Ilkeston North in 1950 and closed to passengers in September 1964. Freight traffic continued until 1968.

A Fletton–Kidderminster sugar beet train passes through the closed West Hallam station in 1967, hauled by a Class 25. West Hallam was originally called Stanley. (RCTS)

The GNR station in Derby was at Friargate. A view of the station in LNER days, taken from the roof of the adjacent goods warehouse.

The goods yard and warehouse.

A view of the goods warehouse from the other end, taken in 1991. Despite being a listed building the warehouse has suffered considerable damage since this photograph was taken, losing most of its roof.

On 28 June 1952 Johnson 5-foot 3-inch 0-4-4T No. 58087 stands at Friargate at the head of the SLS Midlands Branch special train. Built in 1900, No. 58087 was finally withdrawn in 1955.

The platforms at Friargate in 1991. In 1939 Friargate effectively became the western terminus of the line from Nottingham and Grantham, regular passenger services to stations further west having ended in that year, although freight and excursion traffic continued. In 1947 there were eleven services on weekdays between Nottingham and Derby Friargate.

A post-war view of Etwall station.

Etwall signal box seen in 1991. Following complete closure in 1968 the line as far as Mickleover was acquired for research. This work ceased in 1990 and the track was lifted shortly before this photograph was taken.

At Egginton Junction a new joint station was built. Beyond Egginton the GNR had running powers to Bromshall Junction, and by the purchase of the Stafford & Uttoxeter Railway in 1881 were able to run trains as far as Stafford. These are the NSR platforms looking towards Derby.

A branch from Ilkeston to Shipley, initially for coal traffic, was opened in June 1886. This was extended to Heanor in July 1891. The station was known unofficially as Heanor Gate to distinguish it from the MR station. In 1950 it was renamed Heanor South. Passenger services were withdrawn in 1939. It is pictured many years after closure.

The GNR's only other penetration into Derbyshire was the northern end of the Leen Valley Extension, opened on 1 November 1901. The line was built for coal traffic and passenger traffic was never important. There were just two stations in Derbyshire, at Pleasley East and Shirebrook South. Passenger services were withdrawn in September 1931. An early photograph of Pleasley Colliery. Notice the private owner wagons in the foreground. The colliery ceased production in 1986 and is being developed as a heritage site. It is a Scheduled Ancient Monument.

The North Staffordshire Railway

Authorised in 1846, the North Staffordshire Railway opened its line from Uttoxeter to Burton-on-Trent on 11 September 1848 and to Willington Junction on the B&DJ on 13 July 1849. There were four intermediate stations: Marchington, Sudbury, Scropton and Tutbury. The NSR always considered the line to Derby the main route with the line to Burton as a branch. Scropton closed as early as 1866. On 28 April 1991 a Class 108 approaches Scropton Crossing with the 13.10 Nottingham to Crewe.

Tutbury closed in 1966 but a new station, Tutbury and Hatton, opened on 3 April 1989. The signal box is a McKenzie and Holland type 1 and dates from 1872. It is listed Grade II. In 1953 Tutbury saw nine services in each direction on weekdays. In the summer months there were additional services on Saturdays conveying through carriages to a number of North Wales destinations. The shuttle service from Tutbury to Burton ceased in 1960.

The Peak Forest Tramway

This 6-mile tramway was constructed by Benjamin Outram, who also built the Peak Forest Canal, with which the tramway connected at Bugsworth Basin. It was built to transport limestone from Doveholes to the basin, where it was either transhipped to the canal or burnt in local limekilns. The single track, later doubled, was built to a gauge of 4 feet 2 inches, the L-shaped rails being laid on stone blocks. The tramway relied on horsepower but there was also a rope-worked incline at Chapel-en-le-Frith. The tramway opened on 31 August 1796. In 1846 it was leased by the Sheffield, Ashton & Manchester Railway and closed in 1924. Bugsworth Basin is seen here in around 1920.

The same view in 2020. The building has gone but the view is recognisably the same. In the foreground are the stone blocks on which the rails were laid.

At Barmoor Clough the tramway ran alongside the LNW Manchester–Buxton line, which passed through the left hand arch of the bridge, the tramway passing through the right-hand side. (J.W. Sutherland)

The Ashover Light Railway

The ALR was the last narrow gauge railway built by Colonel Stephens. It was built to serve a number of quarries and an opencast coal mine. It ran from Clay Cross to Ashover Butts. The line was built to a 60-cm gauge using war surplus material. Construction started in December 1922 and was completed by the spring of 1924. The terminus at Ashover Butts is shown here.

The motive power and rolling stock were also derived from war surplus material. The company purchased four Baldwin 4-6-0Ts and a number of Hudson open bogie wagons. The four carriages supplied by the Gloucester Carriage & Wagon Company were also built on Hudson bogies. Bridget, one of the Baldwins, is seen here. The locomotives were named after the children of the general manager of the Clay Cross Company.

Passenger traffic started on 6 April but regular trains only lasted until 1931. After that, special trains continued to run on Sundays and bank holidays. The main traffic for the railway was ballast for the LMS. Following nationalisation in 1948 and the loss of the contract to supply ballast, the railway went into terminal decline and closed completely in 1950. A train being turned on the triangle at Ashover Butts is seen here.